The Brevelle Toasted Sandwiches Book

JUDY RIDGWAY

A Martin Book

Published by Martin Books
17 Market Street, Cambridge CB2 3PA
in association with Breville Europe Limited
Alexandra House, Alexandra Terrace
Guildford, Surrey GU1 3DA

First published 1982

© Breville Europe Limited and Judy Ridgway 1982

ISBN 0 85941 189 3

Design: Ken Vail Graphic Design
Photography: John Lee
Typeset by Clavier Spools, Southend-on-Sea, Essex
Printed in Great Britain by Balding + Mansell
Wisbech, Cambs

Foreword

by Colin Cookman
Managing Director, Breville Europe Limited

When we consumer-tested the Snack 'n' Sandwich Toaster in June 1978 we knew from the very positive response across the country that we had a product with considerable potential. In the event the response was way beyond our most optimistic forecasts, and within the space of 3 years it has become the fastest-selling small appliance in the country.

How did this happen? There are many contributory factors but the main reason, I believe, is that the sandwich toaster creates a new type of snack – a toasted sandwich with a sealed-in filling that can be made from anything in just a couple of minutes.

I am delighted that Judy Ridgway – along with many thousands of Breville users – found her Snack 'n' Sandwich Toaster even more useful than she had perhaps anticipated. I have to admit that many of her imaginative and delicious recipes had not even occurred to us and so I am sure that this book will help you make the most of your Breville Snack 'n' Sandwich Toaster.

Colin Cookman.

Contents

Introduction 6

How to Use and Care for
   your Breville Snack 'n'
   Sandwich Toaster 7
Using your Breville Snack 'n'
   Sandwich Toaster 7
Caring for your Breville Snack
   'n' Sandwich Toaster 8

Hints and Tips for Better
   Brevilles 10
Bread 10
Dipped Bread 10
Pastry and Pizza Linings 11
Butters 11
Sweet Coatings 12
Presentation 12
Using Leftovers 13

Family Favourites 16
Mushroom and Bacon
   Delights 16
West Indian Chicken
   Brevilles 17
Cheese Gems 17
Egg and Aubergine Layered
   Brevilles 18
Prawn and Sesame
   Sandwiches 20
Smoky Barbecue 20
French Connection 21
Italian Dreams 22
Peanut Butter Scallops 22

Chilli Bean Toasties 24
Cod and Parsley Supper 24
Old English 25
Carrot Croquettes 25
Seafood Rolls 26
Meat Patties 28

Made in a Moment 29
Mexican Omelettes 29
Minty Pineapple 30
Tuna Treats 30
Herby Ham Omelettes 32
Tasty Tongue 32
Chicken and Asparagus
   Brevilles 33
Peanut Patties 33
Italian Layered Brevilles 34
Cheese Dreams 36
Cheese and Carrot
   Dreams 36
Cheese and Apple Dreams 36
Brie and Mushroom
   Dreams 37
Cheese and Chutney
   Dreams 37
Dijon Dreams 38
Blue Cheese Dreams 38

Sweet Brevilles 39
Date and Walnut Slices 39
Madeira Magic 40
Jam Omelettes 40
Summer Specials 41
Ice Cream Brevilles 41

Jamaican Treats 42
Orange Caprice 42
Melon and Ginger
   Brevilles 44
Gooseberry Turnovers 44
Banana and Date Delights 45
Black Forest Brevilles 45
Pear Hélène 46
Indian Dreams 46
Tangy Madeira Slices 48
Turkish Delights 48

Children's Choice 50
Apple and Raspberry
   Turnovers 50
Cheesy Choice 51
Sausage Supper 51
Alphabet Toasties 52
Triple Deckers 52
Beef Bullets 53
Peanut Surprise 54
Corn Dogs 54
Hot Dog Brevilles 56
Curried Brevilles 56
Chocolate Nut Krispies 57
Dutch Delights 58
Boston Brevilles 58

Breakfasts 60
Breakfast Brevilles 60
Ham and Egg Breakfast 61
Smoky Brunch 61
Devilled Mushroom
   Brevilles 62
Chocolate Bread 64
Sweet Egg Toasties 64
Kipper Delights 65
Bury Breakfast 65
Stuffed Oatcakes 1 66
Stuffed Oatcakes 2 67

**Pizzas, Pastries and
   Pasties 68**
Pizza Dough 68

Basic Pizza Dough 68
Basic Tomato Sauce 69
Vesuvio 69
Capri 70
Pompeii 70
Milano 72
Samosa Dough 73
Basic Samosa Dough 73
Bombay 73
Peking 74
Singapore 76
Shortcrust and Puff Pastry 76
Salmon Pasties 77
Cock-a-leekie Pies 77
Morecambe Magic 78
Cornish Pasties 80
Apple Pies 80
Choux Pastry 81
Basic Choux Pastry 81
Hot Choux Melba 81
Savoury Choux Rolls 82
Choux Splits 82

Party Specials 85
Toasted Cocktail Sandwiches 85
Prawn and Avocado
   Canapés 85
Smoked Salmon and Egg
   Canapés 86
Duck and Orange
   Canapés 86
Chicken Liver Canapés 88
Smoky Gems 89
Savoury Whirls 90
Garlic and Parsley Whirls 90
Liver and Sage Whirls 92
Smoky Whirls 92
Spiced Herring Whirls 93
More Substantial Fingers 93
Asparagus Fingers 93
Mock Caviare Fingers 94
Breville Kebabs 96

Introduction

I can honestly say that I became a Breville addict the first day the toasted sandwich machine arrived in my kitchen. I started off with a simple toasted cheese and bacon Breville and I was hooked for life. Since then I have tried out all kinds of different mixtures and they have all taken well to this method of cooking. I have also experimented with flavoured butters and dipped breads and tried out pastry and pizza linings. I even discovered that choux pastry is lighter and fluffier when cooked in a toasted sandwich maker than when cooked in the oven!

I have found that Brevilles are both quick and easy to make and that they fit very well into the lifestyle of the modern family. The same piece of equipment can be used for rustling up instant fillers for hungry teenagers, for making light lunches and TV snacks, for producing gourmet-style starters for special dinners and for making exciting party canapés.

This book is a collection of my favourite Breville recipes. They are all suitable for both the SG3 Snack 'n' Sandwich Toaster and the 8-Up Snack 'n' Sandwich Toaster. Follow *either* the metric (g, ml) *or* the imperial (oz, pint) measures, *but never a mixture of both,* in any recipe and remember that all the spoon measures refer to level measures unless otherwise stated.

I do hope that you all have as much fun with your new machine as I have had with mine and that this book will stimulate you to think of all sorts of new ideas for linings, flavourings and fillings.

How to Use and Care for your Breville Snack 'n' Sandwich Toaster

You are sure to want to try out your Breville Snack 'n' Sandwich Toaster as soon as you get it home, so just unpack it from its box, brush over the inside scallops with vegetable oil before using it for the first time, and you are ready to go.

Using your Breville Snack 'n' Sandwich Toaster
Plug in the appliance, close the lid and switch on the power. The red indicator light will come on and will remain on until the power is switched off. I find this a very useful reminder to switch off the appliance after I have made a batch of Brevilles.

You will need to preheat your Snack 'n' Sandwich Toaster for about 5 minutes before putting the sandwiches in and this time can be used to assemble the ingredients and to butter the bread. Of course, if you are trying out one of the more elaborate recipes in this book, you may need to get the filling on the go before switching on the toaster.

When the Breville has reached the correct temperature for you to start toasting, the green indicator light will come on. During toasting, this light will switch on and off, indicating that the correct temperature is being maintained. Lay the bread on the preheated scallops and place the filling on top. I find that the best results are obtained by lightly buttering the bread and placing it buttered side down on the scallops. The second piece of bread is also placed with its buttered side against the scallops. This gives more of a fried bread effect and the resulting Brevilles come out a lovely deep golden colour with a crispy texture. Of course, if you are on a diet you may want to cut down on butter. This is no problem as the bread can be used unbuttered, but you may need to re-oil the scallops after toasting a number of sandwiches in this way. The scallops may also need to be oiled for pastry linings and for doughs, croquettes and patties. However, instructions are given in the recipes for these types of Brevilles.

The amount of filling required in your Brevilles depends on the thickness of the lining and on whether or not they are to be turned across the cutting bars halfway through cooking to make mini or cocktail sandwiches. Obviously, if you are using thick slices of bread there will be less room for the filling. I prefer to use medium sliced bread and to roll out pastries and doughs as thinly as possible. The quantities given in the following recipes reflect this preference. You may need to use a little less filling if you decide to make them into cocktail sandwiches as these have a greater tendency to burst if filled too full.

On the other hand, it is also important to make sure that the sandwiches have enough filling – a heaped tablespoonful is usually about the right amount. Brevilles using sliced meats will need some other ingredients like sliced tomato, chutney or relish to push the outside of the bread against the scallops and so ensure even toasting.

Once the filling is in place, cover with the remaining bread, buttered side up and lower the lid to start toasting. With sliced meats or raw food, lower the lid slowly. This enables the scissor action to work efficiently. Latch the handles together and toast for about 2 minutes. Toasting is really a matter of taste, but I find that this is ample time to give the sort of good crispy texture and golden colour that I like. The filling will also be well heated through the middle. In fact, food like cheese and jam are so hot that care is needed in eating them.

Some Brevilles take rather longer to cook. These have pastry or dough linings or no linings at all and for these the handles of the appliance should not be latched together.

When the toasting or cooking time is complete, release the latch and open the lid. Use a nylon or wooden spatula to remove the Brevilles. Never use a metal utensil as this can damage the non-stick coating.

Caring for your Breville Snack 'n' Sandwich Toaster
Remember to switch off the power and unplug the Breville as soon as you have finished using it. Leave the appliance to

cool until it is warm but not hot and then wipe over the inside with kitchen towel or a soft cloth. The outside can be cleaned by wiping over with a cloth which has been squeezed out in warm, soapy water. Finish off with a soft, dry cloth.

In most cases this is all that is needed to keep the Breville in good condition. However, if you over-fill the sandwiches, the filling may ooze out on to the scallops. To remove this, simply pour a little cooking oil on the baked-on food and leave to stand for 5–10 minutes. This will soften the food and make it much easier to remove. If this still doesn't work, try a little detergent. Leave to stand again and then wipe off with a soft cloth or a plastic scourer. Whatever you do, don't use steel wool, scouring pads or abrasive cleaners. This will damage the non-stick coating on the inside and lead to food sticking more frequently and will also badly scratch the outside finish.

Hints and Tips for Better Brevilles

Plain filled Brevilles are excellent but you may want to have a change, to pep up otherwise plain ingredients or to give a festive flavour to your favourite recipe. This can be done quite easily by varying the kind of bread you use, by dipping the bread in egg or flavoured milk, by using flavoured butters and by paying extra attention to presentation.

Bread
Most kinds of bread can be used for making Brevilles but the size of the slice is important and should cover a whole scallop. A medium sliced long loaf of white or wholemeal bread is the most convenient bread to use but there is no reason why you should not cut the required size slice off any loaf (each slice should be approximately 10 cm/4 in square). Raisin bread, milk bread and light rye bread all work well, although raisin bread may toast a bit faster than the others, and be careful with black bread as this may become hard when cooked. There is no need to remove the crusts unless they are very tough or crisp, though I do like to cut them off for cocktail sandwiches and party fare.

Dipped Bread
Different textures and flavours can be obtained by dipping the bread in egg or flavoured milk. These Brevilles are not as crisp as undipped ones but some of my friends prefer them to the regular variety. One small egg, well beaten, is usually sufficient for dipping four slices of bread. It can be seasoned with salt and pepper and flavoured with a variety of herbs and spices. Tarragon is a particular favourite of mine but paprika or grated orange rind for sweet Brevilles are popular with my family.

Dipped bread Brevilles take a little longer to toast than

undipped ones, so allow about 4 minutes' cooking time and remember to oil the scallops if you are cooking a large batch.

Pastry and Pizza Linings

Pastry and pizza doughs work well as Breville linings. Both shortcrust and puff pastry can be used, as can samosa and pizza dough (see recipes on pages 68–84). These linings tend to shrink on contact with the hot scallops and so need to be cut into 13 cm/5 in squares. They also take a little longer to cook than bread, but you will find full instructions given with each recipe.

Butters

For simplicity I have usually suggested brushing Brevilles with butter, but most kinds of fat can be used. Quantities will of course vary with the number of Brevilles you are making. However, it is better to use too little rather than too much fat as any excess will run out and make the outside of the appliance and the working surface greasy.

The butter can also be flavoured for added interest. Ideas I have tried include the following, but I am sure that you will be able to come up with some more.

Garlic Butter:	Add crushed garlic and salt and pepper.
Tomato Butter:	Add tomato purée and tomato ketchup and pepper.
Parsley Butter:	Add very finely chopped fresh parsley, salt and a pinch of cayenne pepper.
Herb Butter:	Add finely chopped fresh or dried herbs on their own or make up your own mixtures.
Celery Butter:	Add celery salt and black pepper.
Mustard Butter:	Add your favourite mustard and salt and pepper.
Fruit Butter:	Add a little lemon or orange juice and finely grated rind.
Anchovy Butter:	Add a very finely chopped anchovy or a little anchovy essence and some black pepper.
Barbecue Butter:	Add a little Worcestershire sauce, tomato ketchup, vinegar and sugar.

Curry Butter:	Add curry powder to taste or a mixture of ground cumin, coriander and crushed cardamoms.
Chilli Butter:	Add ground chilli powder or very finely chopped green chillis with the seeds removed.
Sweet and Sour Butter:	Add sieved chutney, a little vinegar and salt and pepper.

In each case, cream the flavouring into the butter to form a smooth paste. Any excess can be stored in the fridge. All these flavoured butters can be used for making hot savoury whirls (see pages 90–93).

Sweet Coatings
A sprinkling of sugar on the buttered side of the bread makes sweet Brevilles crisper and sweeter. Alternatively, make up sugar-flavoured butters with icing sugar and a little fruit juice, brandy, rum or your favourite liqueur. Spices like cinnamon, nutmeg or mixed spice also taste delicious with the butter and icing sugar mixture.

Presentation
Like all food, Brevilles are at their best if they are well presented and a small garnish of tomato and watercress or mayonnaise and wedges of lemon can turn even a humble filler into a gourmet snack. Brevilles can also make an interesting starter to a main meal and presentation is even more important here.

Obviously, the garnish will depend on what is in the Breville, but here are a few general ideas to point the way.

| *Fish Brevilles:* | Wedges of lemon or lemon sauce, tartare sauce, parsley or parsley sauce, tomatoes stuffed with peas, or rounds of herb butter. |
| *Meat Brevilles:* | Tomato florets (tomatoes that have been cut round to the centre in a zig-zag pattern and separated in half) and watercress, relishes and chutneys, tomato sauce or gravy, or salads. |

Pastry Brevilles:	Tomato or barbecue sauce, hollandaise or flavoured mayonnaise sauce, soya sauce or salads.
Savoury Whirls:	Mustard or piquant tomato dips.
Sweet Brevilles:	Whipped cream, ice cream, fruit, apricot, raspberry or chocolate sauce, jam or honey.

Brevilles can also be served with soup to make a light but nourishing meal. Good combinations include Italian Layered Brevilles with minestrone soup, Mushroom and Bacon Delights with a good vegetable soup, Chilli Bean Toasties or Hot Dog Brevilles with tomato soup and Alphabet Toasties with chicken soup.

Garnishing and serving suggestions are also given with some of the recipes.

Using Leftovers

I hate throwing away those small quantities of leftovers from special dinners or Sunday lunch and now I have a marvellous way of using them up. They are ideal for making quick Breville fillings and I have achieved all sorts of exotic mixtures simply by teaming them up with ingredients that I have found in the fridge or store cupboard.

In addition to the leftover food you will almost always need some complementary ingredients, some flavourings and something to bind the whole together. Leftover duck, for example, is delicious with apple sauce or sage and onion stuffing, chicken goes well with fruit, and cold beef or lamb is good with fried onion, relish or leftover potatoes. If you want to give your Brevilles extra flavour try adding some chilli or curry powder or fresh herbs. For binding use cream cheese, mayonnaise, leftover sauces or gravy.

Stale cake and biscuits can be soaked in fruit juice or alcohol (such as brandy, rum, sherry or fruit liqueur) and used as fillings in sweet Brevilles and those bits of French and Italian cheese from the dinner party cheese board can be teamed up with tomato, cucumber or celery.

Leftovers also form the basis of good patties and croquettes. These can be cooked in the Breville without any lining of bread or pastry. Bind the ingredients together with left-over sauce, mashed potatoes or beaten egg. The latter can also be used to dip the croquettes just before cooking and a light coating of flour before dipping will help to hold the egg in place. Preheat the scallops in the normal way, shape the croquette mixture to fit the scallops and lay them in place. Close the lid but do not latch the handle and cook for 4–8 minutes depending on the mixture. Some patty and croquette recipes are given in the Family Favourites section (see pages 16–28).

Prawn and Sesame Sandwiches

Family Favourites

A well-filled Breville served with soup or a salad makes a good second meal for the family and I often serve them for a quick lunch after doing the weekend shopping on a Saturday morning or as a TV supper when we plan to watch a long film. Some of the fillings take a little preparation but it is worth spending just a short time making a filling that will provide fairly substantial nourishment.

Mushroom and Bacon Delights
Makes 4

This delicious combination is great for an evening at home, but go easy on the garlic if you are going out!

4 lean rashers bacon
100 g/4 oz mushrooms, sliced
25 g/1 oz butter
1–2 cloves garlic, crushed
4 slices bread

Grill the bacon until cooked to your liking. Cut each rasher in half and drain off the fat. Gently fry the mushrooms in a very little butter until they soften. Drain off any liquid which accumulates. Mix the remaining butter with the garlic and spread on one side of each slice of bread. Lay two slices of bread, buttered side down, on to the preheated scallops. Lay a piece of bacon over each scallop and spoon a quarter of the mushrooms on to each piece of bacon. Cover with a second piece of bacon and top with the remaining slices of bread, buttered side up. Lower the lid and toast for 2 minutes.

West Indian Chicken Brevillés
Makes 4   (Pictured on the front cover)

Buy a cooked chicken breast or use leftovers from the weekend chicken to make this unusual fruity-flavoured Breville.

75 g/3 oz cream cheese
75 g/3 oz cooked chicken, diced
2 slices canned pineapple, finely chopped
¼ small green pepper, very finely chopped
salt and pepper
4 slices bread, buttered on one side

Beat the cream cheese to a smooth paste with a fork and mix in the chicken, pineapple, green pepper and seasonings. Lay two slices of bread, buttered side down, on the preheated scallops. Divide the cream cheese and chicken mixture between the two and cover with the remaining slices of bread, buttered side up. Lower the lid and toast for 2 minutes.

Cheese Gems
Makes 4   (Pictured on page 19)

Cheese Gems made with bread dipped in egg have a soft, light texture, but they are just as good made with plain buttered bread.

100 g/4 oz courgettes, thinly sliced
15 g/½ oz butter
5 ml spoon/1 teaspoon tomato purée
garlic salt and pepper
4 slices bread, buttered on one side with Herb Butter (see
    page 11)
1 large egg, beaten
25 g/1 oz Cheddar or Emmenthal cheese, grated

Gently fry the courgettes in butter for 4–5 minutes until they are softened. Stir in the tomato purée and seasoning.

Dip two slices of bread in beaten egg and lay them on top of the preheated scallops. Add the courgette mixture and the cheese. Dip the remaining slices of bread in the rest of the egg and use to cover the Brevilles. Lower the lid and toast for 4 minutes. Serve with tomato sauce or ketchup.

Egg and Aubergine Layered Brevilles
Makes 8

All kinds of quickly cooked vegetables lend themselves to this kind of recipe. Try substituting courgettes or green peppers for the aubergines. Alternatively, you could try using up leftover carrots, potatoes or cauliflower.

50 g/2 oz butter
1 aubergine, sliced
3–4 × 15 ml spoon/3–4 tablespoons flour seasoned with salt and pepper
1 egg, beaten
5 ml spoon/1 teaspoon tomato purée
8 slices bread
2 tomatoes, sliced
2.5 ml spoon/½ teaspoon dried oregano

Melt half the butter in a pan. Dip the slices of aubergine in the seasoned flour and then in the egg. Fry in the hot butter for about 3–4 minutes on each side until tender. Mix the rest of the butter with the tomato purée and spread on one side of each slice of bread. Lay two or four slices of bread, buttered side down, on the preheated scallops. Cover with slices of aubergine and slices of tomato and sprinkle with oregano. Top with slices of bread, buttered side up. Lower the lid and toast for 2 minutes. Repeat with the remaining ingredients if necessary.

Egg and Aubergine Layered Brevilles; Cheese Gems

Prawn and Sesame Sandwiches
Makes 4   (Pictured on page 15)

Sesame-coated buns are popular for hamburgers and the same effect can be achieved by sprinkling Brevilles with sesame seeds before toasting. Remember to wipe any excess seeds off the toaster after use.

100 g/4 oz peeled prawns, chopped
1 hard-boiled egg, chopped
a little mayonnaise
salt and pepper
4 slices bread, buttered on one side
5 ml spoon/1 teaspoon sesame seeds

Mix the prawns and hard-boiled egg and moisten with the mayonnaise. Season to taste. Sprinkle the buttered side of the bread with sesame seeds and press the seeds into the butter with a knife. Lay two slices of bread, buttered side down on the preheated scallops. Spoon the egg and prawn mixture on to the top and cover with the remaining slices of bread, buttered side up. Lower the lid and toast for 2–3 minutes.

Smoky Barbecue
Makes 4   (Pictured on the front cover)

English or Austrian smoked cheese can be used for this recipe, but the Austrian gives a more stringy effect.

4 slices bread, spread with cold bacon fat
50 g/2 oz English or Austrian smoked cheese, sliced or
   grated
2 × 5 ml spoon/2 teaspoons barbecue or Worcestershire
   sauce
2 × 10 cm/4 in squares cooked ham *or* 4 rashers cooked
   smoked bacon

Lay two slices of bread, fat side down, on the preheated

scallops. Spoon on the cheese and sprinkle with your chosen sauce. Top with slices of ham or bacon and cover with bread, buttered side up. Lower the lid and toast for 2 minutes.

French Connection
Makes 8   (Pictured on page 31)

Freshly made, leftover or canned ratatouille can be used in this very French-flavoured Breville. However, if you don't have all the ingredients to hand courgettes, peppers or aubergines fried with tomatoes and onion make an excellent alternative.

1 small onion, chopped
15 ml spoon/1 tablespoon cooking oil
1 courgette, sliced
½ green or red pepper, seeded and sliced
½ small aubergine, chopped
3 tomatoes, chopped
5 ml spoon/1 teaspoon tomato purée
1.25 ml spoon/¼ teaspoon dried thyme
salt and pepper
3–4 × 15 ml spoon/3–4 tablespoons white wine, cider or tomato juice
8 slices bread, buttered on one side
50 g/2 oz Gruyère cheese, grated

Fry the onion in cooking oil until it turns transparent. Add the remaining vegetables and gently fry for 2–3 minutes. Add the tomato purée, thyme, seasoning and wine, cider or tomato juice and bring to the boil. Reduce the heat and simmer for about 30 minutes until all the liquid has been taken up and the vegetables are tender. Lay two or four pieces of bread, buttered side down, on the preheated scallops and place 15 ml spoon/1 tablespoon of ratatouille over each scallop. Sprinkle with cheese and cover with slices of bread, buttered side up. Lower the lid and toast for 2 minutes. Repeat with the remaining ingredients if necessary. Serve with a green salad.

Italian Dreams
Makes 4

Spinach and cream cheese are often used in Italy to stuff pancakes or little pasta envelopes and the mixture is equally good in toasted sandwiches. Use full fat soft cheese for a smooth effect or cottage cheese for a coarser, more speckly look.

$\frac{1}{2}$ × 250 g/8$\frac{1}{2}$ oz packet frozen chopped spinach
225 g/8 oz cream cheese or cottage cheese
salt and black pepper
pinch of nutmeg
4 slices bread, buttered on one side

Thaw the spinach and squeeze out as much liquid as possible. Beat the cream cheese with a fork to soften it (or, if you are using cottage cheese, to break down the lumps) and mix in the spinach. Season with plenty of salt, black pepper and nutmeg. Lay two slices of bread, buttered side down, on the preheated scallops. Divide the spinach and cream cheese mixture between the two and top with the remaining slices of bread, buttered side up. Lower the lid and toast for 2 minutes. Serve sprinkled with Parmesan cheese.

Peanut Butter Scallops
Makes 4

I think crunchy peanut butter gives a more interesting texture to these very quick snacks.

350 g/12 oz mashed potatoes
4 × 5 ml spoon/1$\frac{1}{2}$ tablespoons peanut butter
salt and pepper

Italian Dreams

Mix all the ingredients together and shape into four croquettes to fit the scallops. Place on the preheated scallops and lower the lid without latching. Cook for 4 minutes. Serve with a few sprigs of watercress.

Chilli Bean Toasties
Makes 8

The secret of a good chilli bean recipe is not so much the chilli as the cumin powder. This unusual spice adds a very special flavour to the recipe.

213 g/7½ oz can minced beef with onions
2.5 ml spoon/½ teaspoon ground cumin
1–2 × 2.5 ml spoon/½–1 teaspoon ground chilli, to taste
350 g/12 oz cooked red kidney beans, well drained
8 slices bread, buttered on one side

Mix the minced beef with the spices and stir in the beans. Place two or four slices of bread, buttered side down, on the preheated scallops. Spoon on the beef mixture and cover with slices of bread, buttered side up. Lower the lid and toast for 2 minutes. Repeat with the remaining ingredients if necessary. Serve with a green salad.

Cod and Parsley Supper
Makes 6

Take care when eating this deliciously fishy Breville as the filling tends to spurt out. If you like you can add a little diced, cooked potato. This will take up some of the sauce at the same time as stretching the ingredients to make eight Brevilles.

2 × 170 g/6 oz packets frozen cod steaks in parsley sauce
6 slices bread, buttered on one side

Cook the cod as directed on the pack. Drain the fish into a basin and mash with a fork. Mix the mashed fish into the sauce. Lay two or three slices of bread, buttered side down, on the preheated scallops. Spoon on the fish mixture and cover with slices of bread, buttered side up. Lower the lid and toast for 2 minutes. Repeat with the remaining ingredients if necessary. Serve with grilled tomatoes and a green salad.

Old English
Makes 4   (Pictured on page 31)

The traditional combination of ham and peas dates from way back in the culinary past. I like it with thyme and tarragon but you could experiment with different herbs.

75 g/3 oz cream cheese
50 g/2 oz cooked peas
75 g/3 oz ham, finely chopped
1.25 ml spoon/¼ teaspoon dried thyme
pinch of dried tarragon
salt and pepper
4 slices bread, buttered on one side

Beat the cream cheese with a fork to soften it and mix in the peas and ham. Add the herbs and season to taste. Lay two slices of bread, buttered side down, on the preheated scallops. Divide the Old English mixture between the two and top with the remaining slices of bread, buttered side up. Lower the lid and toast for 2 minutes.

Carrot Croquettes
Makes 4   (Pictured on page 27)

Any leftover vegetables can be substituted for carrots in this recipe if you wish. Choose a flavouring to complement the chosen vegetable.

225 g/8 oz cooked carrots, mashed
350 g/12 oz mashed potato
a little beaten egg or mayonnaise to bind
2.5 ml spoon/½ teaspoon cumin powder *or* 1.25 ml spoon/¼
    teaspoon ground black pepper
cooking oil

Mix together all the ingredients except the cooking oil and shape the mixture to fit the scallops. If using mayonnaise to bind, brush the preheated scallops with a little oil. Place the croquettes in the scallops. Lower the lid but do not latch and cook for 4–5 minutes.

Seafood Rolls
Makes 4

These make a delicious starter to a meal served with a piquant tomato sauce or an anchovy sauce. Alternatively, they make a good lunchtime snack with salad.

198 g/7 oz can tuna, salmon or mackerel or leftover cooked
    white fish
175 g/6 oz cooked mashed potato
2 × 15 ml spoon/2 tablespoons chopped parsley
2 small eggs, beaten
salt and pepper
flour

Drain the fish and mash it with a fork. Mix with the potato and parsley and bind with about half the beaten egg. Season to taste. Shape into four fat triangles or sausage shapes. Roll in flour and dip in the remaining beaten egg. Place on the preheated scallops, lower the lid without latching and cook for about 5 minutes until golden on the outside.

Seafood Rolls; Meat Patties; Carrot Croquettes

Meat Patties

Makes 4   (Pictured on page 27)

This is a delicious way of using up any leftover meat and you can vary the flavour by adding chilli, curry or ketchup.

350 g/12 oz cooked lamb, beef, pork, chicken or turkey, minced
50 g/2 oz breadcrumbs
2 eggs, beaten
salt and pepper
5 ml spoon/1 teaspoon mixed herbs

Mix all the ingredients together in a basin. Shape into four fat triangles or sausage shapes and place on the preheated scallops. Lower the lid without latching and cook for 3–4 minutes until golden brown. Serve with a little gravy and green vegetables or a salad.

Made in a Moment

A quickly made snack is sometimes all that I have time for and all the recipes in this chapter can be rustled up very quickly indeed. The ingredients are all things which you are quite likely to have in the kitchen already. If not, just look to the store cupboard, the vegetable rack and the fridge for further inspiration.

Mexican Omelettes
Makes 4

If you like a real bite to your food, this Mexican mixture is the quick snack for you.

2 eggs, beaten
milk
butter
2 × 15 ml spoon/2 tablespoons Mexicorn (corn with sweet peppers)
pinch of allspice
1–2 × 2.5 ml spoon/½–1 teaspoon chilli powder *or* 1 fresh chilli, seeded and chopped
4 slices bread, buttered on one side

Very lightly scramble the eggs with a little milk and butter. When the eggs begin to set, stir in the Mexicorn, allspice and chilli. Lay two slices of bread, buttered side down, on the preheated scallops. Divide the egg and corn mixture between the two and top with the remaining slices of bread, buttered side up. Lower the lid and toast for 2 minutes.

Minty Pineapple
Makes 4

The fresh taste of this Breville makes it an excellent snack for a hot summer's day and it looks very attractive served garnished with pineapple and mint.

100 g/4 oz cottage cheese
15 ml spoon/1 tablespoon fresh, chopped mint
salt and pepper
4 slices bread, buttered on one side
227 g/8 oz can pineapple rings

Mix the cottage cheese, mint and seasoning in a basin. Lay two slices of bread, buttered side down, on the preheated scallops. Spoon on the cottage cheese mixture and arrange half a slice of pineapple over each scallop. Cover with the remaining slices of bread, buttered side up, lower the lid and toast for 2 minutes. Serve garnished with the remaining pineapple rings and some sprigs of mint.

Tuna Treats
Makes 4

I have used tuna for these Brevilles, but they are just as tasty made with sardines, pilchards, mackerel or salmon.

99 g/3½ oz can tuna, drained
75 g/3 oz cream cheese or cottage cheese
25 g/1 oz walnuts, finely chopped
salt and pepper
4 slices bread, buttered on one side

Mash the tuna with a fork and add the cream cheese or cottage cheese, walnuts and seasonings. Lay two slices of bread, buttered side down, on the preheated scallops. Spoon the tuna mixture on top and cover with the remaining slices of bread, buttered side up. Lower the lid and toast for 2 minutes.

Tuna Treats; Old English; French Connection

Herby Ham Omelettes
Makes 4

The more egg you can get into this the better, so add a little at a time and if it shows signs of running off the sides let it soak into the bottom layer of bread.

100 g/4 oz ham, chopped
2 small eggs, beaten
salt and pepper
5 ml spoon/1 teaspoon mixed dried herbs
4 slices bread, buttered on one side

Mix the ham, eggs, seasonings and 1.25 ml spoon/¼ teaspoon of mixed herbs in a basin. Sprinkle the buttered side of each slice of bread with the remaining dried herbs. Lay two slices of bread, buttered side down, on the preheated scallops. Carefully spoon on the omelette mixture and top with the remaining slices of bread, buttered side up. Lower the lid and toast for 2–3 minutes.

Tasty Tongue
Makes 4

This is a really quick recipe for which you could use any kind of cold sliced meat.

100 g/4 oz sliced tongue
4 slices bread, buttered on one side
8 × 5 ml spoon/8 teaspoons of your favourite relish or chutney

Cut the tongue into pieces to fit the bread. Lay two slices of bread, buttered side down, on the preheated scallops. Arrange half the tongue on the top. Add 2 × 5 ml spoon/2 teaspoons of relish to each scallop and lay the rest of the tongue on top. Add the remaining two slices of bread, buttered side up. Lower the lid and toast for 2 minutes.

Chicken and Asparagus Brevilles
Makes 4

Canned condensed soup is ideal for pepping up leftovers.
Here I have teamed up asparagus soup with leftover cooked
chicken, but tomato soup and cooked ham, or mushroom
soup and turkey are just as good.

175 g/6 oz diced cooked chicken
2–3 × 15 ml spoon/2–3 tablespoons condensed asparagus
   soup
black pepper
4 slices bread, buttered on one side

Mix the diced chicken, soup and black pepper in a basin,
taking care not to let the mixture get too runny. Lay two
slices of bread, buttered side down, on the preheated scallops. Spoon the chicken mixture into the scallops and top
with the remaining slices of bread, buttered side up. Lower
the lid and toast for 2 minutes. Serve with watercress and
sliced tomatoes.

Peanut Patties
Makes 4

This vitamin-packed Breville is one of my favourite midday
snacks. I always use wholemeal bread and the crunchy kind
of peanut butter.

2 medium-size tomatoes, finely chopped
6 spring onions, finely chopped
2 × 15 ml spoon/2 tablespoons finely chopped parsley
salt and pepper
4 slices of bread, buttered on one side
2 × 15 ml spoon/2 tablespoons peanut butter

Mix the tomatoes, onions and parsley in a basin and season
to taste. Spread the unbuttered side of the bread with peanut
butter and lay two slices, peanut butter side up, on the

preheated scallops. Spoon on the tomato mixture and cover
with the remaining slices of bread, peanut butter side down.
Lower the lid and toast for 2 minutes. Garnish with lettuce
and watercress.

Italian Layered Brevilles
Makes 4

The Italian salami and cheese give this triple-decker Breville
its distinctive taste, but if you can't find them English cer-
velat sausage and Lancashire cheese are almost as good.

75 g/3 oz courgettes, sliced
25 g/1 oz butter
1.25 ml spoon/¼ teaspoon dried oregano or mixed herbs
4 slices bread
8 slices Italian salami
25 g/1 oz Bel Paese cheese

Gently fry the courgettes in a little of the butter until they are
just soft. Mix the remaining butter with the herbs and
spread on to the slices of bread. Spread the salami with the
Bel Paese cheese. Place two slices of bread, buttered side
down, on the preheated scallops. Spoon on the courgettes
and arrange two slices of salami over each scallop. Cover
with the remaining slices of bread, buttered side up. Lower
the lid and toast for 2 minutes.

Cheese Dreams

CHEESE DREAMS   (Pictured on page 35)

The delicious taste and texture of melted cheese lends itself extremely well to the toasted sandwichmaker, but remember to let the sandwich cool a little before eating or you will end up with a burnt tongue! Try experimenting with different kinds of cheese and mix them with chutneys, relishes and sauces. Here are some ideas to set you off.

Cheese and Carrot Dreams
Makes 4   (Pictured on the front cover)

15 g/½ oz butter
1.25 ml spoon/¼ teaspoon dried mixed herbs
4 slices bread
75 g/3 oz Cheddar cheese, grated
75 g/3 oz carrots, grated
2 × 5 ml spoon/2 teaspoons mayonnaise
salt and black pepper

Mix the butter with the herbs and spread on one side of each of the slices of bread. Mix the cheese, carrot, mayonnaise and seasoning. Lay two slices of bread, buttered side down, on the preheated scallops. Spread with the cheese and carrot mixture. Top with the remaining slices of bread, buttered side up, lower the lid and toast for 2 minutes.

Cheese and Apple Dreams
Makes 4

75 g/3 oz Wensleydale or Lancashire cheese, grated
1 small apple, cored and grated
2.5 ml spoon/½ teaspoon coriander, cumin or curry powder
2 × 5 ml spoon/2 teaspoons raisins
4 slices bread, buttered on one side

Mix the cheese, apple, chosen spice and raisins in a bowl. Lay two slices of bread, buttered side down, on the pre-heated scallops. Spread with the cheese and apple mixture. Cover with the remaining slices of bread, buttered side up. Lower the lid and toast for 2 minutes.

Brie and Mushroom Dreams
Makes 4

25 g/1 oz butter
75 g/3 oz mushrooms, sliced
75 g/3 oz Brie, grated
5 ml spoon/1 teaspoon French mustard
4 slices bread

Melt half the butter in a pan and gently fry the mushrooms until tender. Mix with the grated cheese. Mix the mustard with the rest of the butter and spread on one side of each of the slices of bread. Lay two slices, buttered side down, on the preheated scallops. Spread the Brie and mushroom mixture over the top. Cover with the remaining slices of bread, buttered side up, lower the lid and toast for 2 minutes.

Cheese and Chutney Dreams
Makes 4

175 g/6 oz Cheddar, Gloucester, Cheshire or Lancashire
  cheese, grated
15 ml spoon/1 tablespoon chutney
4 slices bread, buttered on one side

Mix the cheese and chutney together in a basin. Lay two slices of bread, buttered side down, on the preheated scallops. Spread each one with half the cheese mixture and cover with the remaining slices of bread, buttered side up. Lower the lid and toast for 2 minutes.

Dijon Dreams
Makes 4

175 g/6 oz hard cheese, grated
2 × 5 ml spoon/2 teaspoons Dijon mustard
3–4 × 5 ml spoon/1–1½ tablespoons beer
4 slices bread, buttered on one side

Mix the cheese and mustard in a basin. Add the beer, taking care not to allow the mixture to get too wet. Lay two slices of bread, buttered side down, on the preheated scallops. Spread with the cheese mixture and cover with the remaining slices of bread, buttered side up. Lower the lid and toast for 2 minutes.

Blue Cheese Dreams
Makes 4

75 g/3 oz Danish Blue, Gorgonzola or Stilton cheese, grated
75 g/3 oz Cheddar cheese, grated
15 g/½ oz walnuts, finely chopped
2 × 5 ml spoon/2 teaspoons mayonnaise
black pepper
4 slices bread, buttered on one side

Mix the cheese, walnuts, mayonnaise and pepper in a basin. Lay two slices of bread, buttered side down, on the preheated scallops. Spread with the cheese mixture and cover with the remaining slices of bread, buttered side up. Lower the lid and toast for 2 minutes.

Sweet Brevilles

The idea of serving hot bread with sweet flavourings is hardly a new one. I adore hot-buttered toast dripping with home-made jam, and bread and butter pudding is high on the list of family favourites, so the idea of sweet fillings for Brevilles caught on immediately. I often make them with sweet flavoured butters to add zest to plainer ingredients and serve them at Sunday lunch. Some of the recipes in this chapter are even grand enough to serve at a special dinner.

Date and Walnut Slices
Makes 4

Any kind of chopped dried fruit can be substituted for dates in this recipe and different kinds of nuts can also be used. Try apricots and almonds, or raisins and peanuts.

50 g/2 oz walnuts, chopped
75 g/3 oz dates, chopped
1–2 × 5 ml spoon/1–2 teaspoons brown sugar to taste
2 × 5 ml spoon/2 teaspoons apricot jam
4 slices bread, buttered on one side
sugar

Mix the walnuts, dates, brown sugar and jam in a basin. Sprinkle the buttered side of the bread with sugar and lay two slices, sugar and butter side down, on the preheated scallops. Spoon on the date and nut mixture and cover with the remaining slices of bread, buttered side up. Lower the lid and toast for 2–3 minutes. Serve with whipped cream.

Madeira Magic
Makes 4

Buy or make the Madeira cake in a large slab, cut it into slices and trim these to the size of the scallops. Take care not to allow the cake to split and remember that it will toast more quickly than bread.

2 × 15 ml spoon/2 tablespoons raisins
2 × 15 ml spoon/2 tablespoons Madeira or sherry
50 g/2 oz ground almonds
5 ml spoon/1 teaspoon sugar
butter
4 slices Madeira cake

Soak the raisins in Madeira or sherry for about 2 hours before using. Add the ground almonds and sugar and mix well together. Butter the slices of cake on one side and lay two of them, buttered side down, on the preheated scallops. Spoon on the raisin mixture and cover with the remaining slices of cake, buttered side up. Lower the lid and toast for 1 minute. Serve at once with double cream.

Jam Omelettes
Makes 4

I like this Breville made with raisin bread but you can use plain white or even wholemeal bread. Ring the changes by using different jams. My favourite is lemon curd.

4 thick slices raisin bread
1 egg, beaten
2 × 15 ml spoon/2 tablespoons jam
sugar

Dip two slices of raisin bread in beaten egg and lay on the preheated scallops. Spread with jam. Dip the remaining slices of bread in the egg and lay on top. Lower the lid and toast for 3–4 minutes. Sprinkle with sugar before serving.

Summer Specials
Makes 4

Everyone who likes strawberries will like these Summer Specials and they are equally good with raspberries or loganberries.

4 slices bread, buttered on one side
sugar
225 g/8 oz strawberries, sliced
8 marshmallows, chopped

Sprinkle the buttered side of the bread with sugar and lay two slices, buttered side down, on the preheated scallops. Arrange the sliced strawberries over the scallops and sprinkle with chopped marshmallows. Cover with the remaining slices of bread, buttered side up. Lower the lid and toast for 2 minutes.

Ice Cream Brevilles
Makes 4

The combination of hot toasted jam sandwich and cold ice cream is popular with all ages. Choose your favourite ice cream and team it up with different jams. I like homemade raspberry jam with raspberry ice cream, but the family favourite is vanilla ice cream and blackcurrant jam.

4 slices white bread or raisin bread, buttered on one side
15 ml spoon/1 tablespoon jam
4 × 15 ml spoon/4 tablespoons ice cream
sugar

Spread the unbuttered side of the bread with jam and lay two slices, buttered side down, on the preheated scallops. Place a spoonful of ice cream over each scallop and quickly cover with the remaining slices of bread, buttered side up. Lower the lid and toast for just 2 minutes. Sprinkle with sugar and serve at once.

Jamaican Treats
Makes 4

These make an excellent ending to a sumptuous dinner. Serve them with cream or ice cream.

2 bananas
15 ml spoon/1 tablespoon dark brown sugar
1–2 × 5 ml spoon/1–2 teaspoons dark rum
15 ml spoon/1 tablespoon raisins
4 slices raisin bread, buttered on one side

Mash the bananas with a fork and mix with brown sugar, rum and raisins. Lay two slices of bread, buttered side down, on the preheated scallops and spoon on the banana mixture. Cover with the remaining bread, buttered side up. Lower the lid and toast for 1–2 minutes.

Orange Caprice
Makes 4

I find this recipe very useful for using up pieces of stale cake and it works just as well with fruit cake as with Madeira or sponge cake.

75 g/3 oz cake crumbs
3 × 5 ml spoon/3 teaspoons orange liqueur
1 small orange, peeled
4 slices bread, buttered on one side
1 egg, beaten

Mix the cake crumbs and liqueur in a basin. Separate the orange segments or cut into slices. Dip two slices of bread in the beaten egg and lay, buttered side down, on the preheated scallops. Spoon on the cake mixture and then add the orange segments or slices. Dip the remaining slices of bread in the rest of the egg and lay on top, buttered side up. Lower the lid and toast for 4 minutes.

Jamaican Treats

Melon and Ginger Brevilles
Makes 4

Mediterranean charantais or cantaloup melons are best for this recipe, but ogen or honeydew melons can be used instead.

4 slices white bread or raisin bread, buttered on one side
½ small melon, peeled, seeded and thinly sliced
2 lumps stem ginger in honey or syrup, thinly sliced
2 × 5 ml spoon/2 teaspoons lime marmalade

Lay two slices of bread, buttered side down, on the pre-heated scallops. Arrange layers of melon and ginger over each scallop and top with a little lime marmalade. Cover with the remaining slices of bread, buttered side up. Lower the lid and toast for 2 minutes. Serve with fresh cream or vanilla ice cream.

Gooseberry Turnovers
Makes 4

My grandmother always used to flavour gooseberries with a handful of elderflowers but these are not very easily available to the modern town dweller so I use a little ginger instead.

283 g/10 oz can gooseberries, drained and puréed
1 lump stem ginger, very finely chopped
4 slices raisin bread, buttered on one side
icing sugar

Mix the gooseberry purée with the stem ginger. Lay two slices of bread, buttered side down, on the preheated scallops. Spoon on the gooseberry mixture and top with the remaining slices of bread, buttered side up. Lower the lid and toast for 1–2 minutes. Serve sprinkled with icing sugar.

Banana and Date Delights
Makes 4

Fresh or dried dates can be used in this recipe. If you use fresh dates, you will probably find that one is sufficient for each Breville.

1 large banana
5 ml spoon/1 teaspoon lemon juice
15 ml spoon/1 tablespoon sugar
4 slices bread, buttered on one side
8 dried dates, halved and stoned, *or* 4 fresh dates, stoned

Mash the banana with a fork and mix with the lemon juice and sugar. Lay two slices of bread, buttered side down, on the preheated scallops and spoon a little of the banana mixture over each scallop. Press four dried date halves or one fresh date into each section and cover with the remaining slices of bread, buttered side up. Lower the lid and toast for 2 minutes. Serve with whipped cream or ice cream.

Black Forest Brevilles
Makes 4   (Pictured on page 47)

If you can get them, fresh cherries can be used for this recipe instead of canned ones.

50 g/2 oz cream cheese
25 g/1 oz sugar
4 slices bread, buttered on one side
225 g/8 oz canned cherries, drained and stoned

Stir together the cream cheese and sugar and spread the mixture over the unbuttered side of the bread. Lay two slices of bread, buttered side down, on the preheated scallops. Press the cherries into the cheese mixture and cover with the remaining slices of bread, buttered side up. Lower the lid and toast for 2 minutes. Serve with vanilla ice cream.

Pear Hélène
Makes 4

Pears with chocolate is one of my favourite flavour combinations and the creamed rice in this recipe gives a lovely rich texture.

1 large pear, peeled, cored and finely chopped
75 g/3 oz creamed rice
25 g/1 oz plain chocolate, grated
4 slices bread, buttered on one side
sugar

Mix the pear, creamed rice and most of the grated chocolate in a basin. Lay two slices of the bread, buttered side down, on the preheated scallops and spoon on the pear and rice mixture. Cover with the remaining bread, buttered side up. Lower the lid and toast for 2 minutes. Remove from the scallops and serve sprinkled with sugar and the remaining chocolate.

Indian Dreams
Makes 4

Cardamom seeds are the main flavouring in a variety of Indian desserts. They go well with milk products and sugar and I have used a similar combination in this sweet Breville.

100 g/4 oz cottage cheese
50 g/2 oz sugar
25 g/1 oz raisins
2–3 cardamom seeds, peeled and crushed
4 slices bread, buttered on one side

Mix the cottage cheese with two thirds of the sugar and add the raisins and crushed cardamoms. Sprinkle the buttered

Black Forest Brevilles; Indian Dreams; Pear Hélène

side of the bread with the remaining sugar and lay two slices, sugared side down, on the preheated scallops. Spoon on the cottage cheese mixture and cover with the remaining bread, buttered side up. Lower the lid and toast for 2 minutes.

Tangy Madeira Slices
Makes 4

I particularly like an old-fashioned tangy marmalade in this Breville as some of the others can be a little too sweet. However, you could try adding a little lemon juice if you have only a sweet marmalade.

4 slices Madeira cake
butter
2 × 15 ml spoon/2 tablespoons marmalade

Cut the slices of Madeira cake to fit the size of the scallops and butter one side of each slice. Place two slices, buttered side down, on the preheated scallops and spread about 3 × 2.5 ml spoon/1½ teaspoons of marmalade over each scallop. Cover with the remaining slices of cake, buttered side up. Lower the lid and toast for 1 minute. Serve with custard.

Turkish Delights
Makes 4

I often serve these lovely almond-flavoured Brevilles at special family meals and at dinner parties and they disappear like hot cakes!

100 g/4 oz almond macaroons, crushed
1–2 × 5 ml spoon/1–2 teaspoons brandy to taste
227 g/8 oz can apricot halves
2 × 5 ml spoon/2 teaspoons sugar
4 slices raisin bread, buttered on one side

Mix the crushed almond macaroons with the brandy and 1–2 × 15 ml spoon/1–2 tablespoons of juice from the apricots. Leave to stand for about 1 hour, until the mixture is soft and mushy. Add a little more of the juice if the mixture is very stiff. Stir in the sugar and spread the mixture over the unbuttered side of the bread. Lay two slices of bread, buttered side down, on the preheated scallops. Arrange two apricot halves over each scallop and cover with the remaining slices of bread, buttered side up. Lower the lid and toast for 1–2 minutes. Serve with whipped cream.

Children's Choice

A child's taste is rarely that of an adult and so I did all my research for this chapter among 7–17 year-olds. All the kids loved baked beans and tomato ketchup but I did manage to get some other ideas out of them as well. Teenagers find Brevilles particularly useful when they are dashing in and out in the evening, and they have also been known to give their own Breville parties!

Apple and Raspberry Turnovers
Makes 4

Almost any kind of fruit purée and any kind of jam can be used in these frequently demanded Brevilles. For instance, try dried apricot purée with marmalade, or gooseberry purée with strawberry jam.

4 × 15 ml spoon/4 tablespoons apple purée
1–2 × 15 ml spoon/1–2 tablespoons soft brown sugar to taste
15 ml spoon/1 tablespoon raspberry jam
4 slices bread, buttered on one side

Mix the apple purée, sugar and jam in a basin. Lay two slices of bread, buttered side down, on the preheated scallops and spoon on the apple and jam mixture. Cover with the remaining slices of bread, buttered side up. Lower the lid and toast for 2 minutes. Serve with custard or cream.

Cheesy Choice
Makes 4

All the children I know seem to be hooked on tomato ketchup and combined with watercress and cheese it can help to encourage healthy eating. Use processed cheese slices if you are in a hurry or try out different English cheeses.

1–2 × 15 ml spoon/1–2 tablespoons tomato ketchup
½ bunch watercress, washed and chopped
4 slices bread, buttered on one side
75 g/3 oz English cheese, finely sliced, *or* 4 slices processed cheese

Mix the ketchup with the chopped watercress. Lay two slices of bread, buttered side down, on the preheated scallops and arrange half the sliced cheese on the top. Spoon on the watercress mixture and add the remaining slices of cheese. Cover with the rest of the bread, buttered side up. Lower the lid and toast for 2 minutes.

Sausage Supper
Makes 4

Any kind of cold cooked sausage can be used in these Brevilles. My favourite is a spiced Cumberland sausage, but you could use beef, pork or even turkey sausages.

3 × 15 ml spoon/3 tablespoons baked beans
5 ml spoon/1 teaspoon Worcestershire sauce
5 ml spoon/1 teaspoon tomato ketchup
1.25 ml spoon/¼ teaspoon thyme
black pepper
4 slices bread, buttered on one side
2 cooked sausages, cut in half lengthways
25 g/1 oz grated cheese (optional)

Mix the baked beans, Worcestershire sauce, tomato ketchup, thyme and black pepper in a basin. Lay two slices of bread, buttered side down, on the preheated scallops. Arrange half a sausage over each scallop and spoon on the bean mixture. Sprinkle with grated cheese, if used, and top with the remaining slices of bread, buttered side up. Lower the lid and toast for 2 minutes.

Alphabet Toasties
Makes 4

These toasties are great fun made with alphabet spaghetti but the long straight variety can be used just as easily.

213 g/7½ oz can alphabet spaghetti in tomato sauce
1 hard-boiled egg, chopped
5 ml spoon/1 teaspoon tomato ketchup
black pepper
4 slices bread, buttered on one side

Mix the spaghetti, hard-boiled egg, ketchup and pepper in a basin. Lay two slices of bread, buttered side down, on the preheated scallops. Spoon on the spaghetti mixture and cover with the remaining slices of bread, buttered side up. Lower the lid and toast for 2 minutes.

Triple Deckers
Makes 4

This is a favourite snack with teenagers. Make sure you have a selection of relishes in the store cupboard and your popularity will be assured!

4 slices bread, buttered on one side
2 slices ham, approx. 10 cm/4 in square
15 ml spoon/1 tablespoon corn relish
2 slices processed cheese
15 ml spoon/1 tablespoon tomato ketchup or tomato-based relish
8 slices salami

Lay two slices of bread, buttered side down, on the preheated scallops. Spread the slices of ham with corn relish and place, relish side up, on the bread. Spread the cheese with the tomato ketchup and place, ketchup side up, on top of the ham. Top with salami and cover with the remaining slices of bread, buttered side up. Lower the lid and toast for 2 minutes.

Beef Bullets
Makes 4

Any kind of cooked and finely chopped meat can be used in these Brevilles but corned beef is still generally the favourite.

1 small onion, finely chopped
15 g/½ oz butter
100 g/4 oz corned beef, very finely chopped
100 g/4 oz mashed potato
salt and pepper
4 slices bread, buttered on one side

Fry the onion in butter until soft and mix it with the corned beef, potato and seasonings. Lay two slices of bread, buttered side down, on the preheated scallops. Spoon some of the beef and potato mixture over each scallop and cover with the remaining slices of bread, buttered side up. Lower the lid and toast for 2 minutes. Serve with baked beans and tomato or a salad.

Peanut Surprise
Makes 4

The hint of sweetness in this savoury Breville is popular with most children. Try it with rhubarb purée or sweet raisin chutney if you want a change.

2 × 15 ml spoon/2 tablespoons peanut butter
2 × 15 ml spoon/2 tablespoons apple purée or sauce
salt and pepper
1 large egg, beaten
4 slices bread, buttered on one side

Mix the peanut butter and apple to a smooth paste. Season the beaten egg and dip two slices of bread in it. Lay these, buttered side down, on the preheated scallops. Place 15 ml spoon/1 tablespoon of the peanut and apple mixture over each scallop. Dip the remaining slices of bread in the rest of the egg and lay on top, buttered side up. Lower the lid and toast for 3–4 minutes.

Corn Dogs
Makes 6

All the family will love these creamy Brevilles but take care to catch the hot drips from the creamed corn.

6 slices bread, buttered on one side
6 hot dog sausages (227 g/8 oz can)
6 × 15 ml spoon/6 tablespoons creamed sweetcorn
salt and pepper

Lay two or three slices of bread, buttered side down, on the preheated scallops. Place a hot dog sausage over each scallop

Chocolate Nut Krispies; Peanut Surprise; Corn Dogs

and top with 15 ml spoon/1 tablespoon of creamed corn. Season to taste. Cover with slices of bread, buttered side up. Lower the lid and toast for 2 minutes. Repeat with the remaining ingredients if necessary.

Hot Dog Brevilles
Makes 6

Hot dog sausages always go down well but you should check that everyone likes mustard.

1 onion, finely sliced
15 ml spoon/1 tablespoon cooking oil
2 tomatoes, roughly chopped
salt and pepper
5 ml spoon/1 teaspoon made mustard *or* 2 × 5 ml spoon/2
　　teaspoons piccalilli, chopped
6 slices bread, buttered on one side
6 hot dog sausages (227 g/8 oz can)

Fry the onion in cooking oil until it turns transparent and then add the tomatoes. Continue cooking until the vegetables are tender. Mix in the seasoning and mustard or piccalilli. Lay two or three slices of bread, buttered side down, on the preheated scallops and place a hot dog sausage over each scallop. Spoon on the onion and tomato mixture and cover with slices of bread. Lower the lid and toast for 2 minutes. Repeat with the remaining ingredients if necessary. Serve with extra mustard or piccalilli.

Curried Brevilles
Makes 4

These Brevilles are very popular and may be made with either specially prepared or leftover vegetables.

3–4 × 5 ml spoon/3–4 teaspoons curry powder
15 g/½ oz butter
4 slices bread
2 small hard-boiled eggs, chopped
50 g/2 oz cooked potatoes, diced
50 g/2 oz cooked vegetables, diced, or cooked peas
2 × 5 ml spoon/2 teaspoons mild chutney or mayonnaise

Mix half the curry powder with the butter and spread on one side of each of the slices of bread. Mix the rest of the ingredients with the remaining curry powder, using chutney or mayonnaise to bind. Lay two slices of bread, buttered side down, on the preheated scallops. Spoon on the curried egg mixture and cover with the remaining slices of bread, buttered side up. Lower the lid and toast for 2 minutes.

Chocolate Nut Krispies
Makes 4   (Pictured on page 55)

Add raisins or chopped glacé cherries to these sweet Brevilles at party time and the plate will empty in a moment.

50 g/2 oz plain chocolate
25 g/1 oz sugar to taste
25 g/1 oz peanuts, walnuts or hazelnuts, chopped
25 g/1 oz Rice Krispies
4 slices bread, buttered on one side

Melt the chocolate in a basin over a bowl of hot water. Stir in two thirds of the sugar, the nuts and the Rice Krispies. Lay two slices of bread, buttered side down, on the preheated scallops. Spoon on the chocolate mixture and cover with the remaining slices of bread, buttered side up. Lower the lid and toast for 2 minutes. Sprinkle with the remaining sugar and some grated chocolate before serving.

Dutch Delights
Makes 4

Gouda cheese gives a good flavour and an interesting stringy texture to these popular Brevilles. Add a couple of slices of tomato in place of the chutney for a change.

4 rashers bacon, grilled and cut in half
4 slices bread, spread on one side with fat from grilling the bacon
4 × 5 ml spoon/4 teaspoons chutney
25 g/1 oz Gouda cheese, grated or cut into thin slices

Lay two slices of bread, fat side down, on the preheated scallops. Arrange two pieces of bacon and 5 ml spoon/1 teaspoon of chutney over each scallop. Top with cheese and cover with the remaining pieces of bread, fat side up. Lower the lid and toast for 2 minutes.

Boston Brevilles
Makes 4

My family are all baked bean addicts and this combination of ham, eggs and baked beans in a favourite midday snack. Boston Brevilles are also good with a little cheese or Worcestershire sauce in place of the ham.

4 slices bread, buttered on one side
1 large egg, beaten
220 g/7¾ oz can baked beans
2 slices ham, approx. 10 cm/4 in square

Dip two of the slices of bread in the beaten egg and lay, buttered side down, on the preheated scallops. Spoon on the baked beans and top with a slice of ham. Dip the remaining slices of bread in the beaten egg and use, buttered side up, to cover the Brevilles. Lower the lid and toast for 3 minutes.

Boston Brevilles; Dutch Delights

Breakfasts

Brevilles make a great all-in-one breakfast. They are quick to prepare and cook and do not leave much mess, which makes them extremely popular with me. It also means that everyone can eat breakfast on a Saturday exactly when they want it.

Breakfast Brevilles
Makes 4   (Pictured on page 63)

Fried leftover potatoes are a favourite in my family and I often prepare extra potatoes for our evening meal to ensure a good supply for the next morning!

2 large rashers bacon, cut in half
25 g/1 oz butter
100 g/4 oz cooked sliced or mashed potatoes
4 slices bread
1 large tomato, sliced
salt and pepper

Fry the bacon in half the butter and then fry the potatoes in the same pan. Drain off any excess fat and spread on the slices of bread with the remaining butter. Lay two slices of bread, buttered side down, on the preheated scallops. Arrange half a rasher of bacon on each scallop. Top with potatoes and tomato and season to taste. Cover with the remaining slices of bread, buttered side up. Lower the lid and toast for 2 minutes. Serve with tomato ketchup or Worcestershire sauce.

Ham and Egg Breakfast
Makes 4

Here is my toasted sandwich version of the traditional English breakfast.

2 eggs, beaten
salt and pepper
4 thick slices bread, buttered on one side
100 g/4 oz ham, sliced

Pour the beaten eggs into a wide soup bowl and season. Dip one slice of bread, buttered side up, in the egg and hold it down for a moment or two. Place on one of the preheated scallops. Repeat with a second slice of bread. Lay slices of ham on each piece of bread. Dip the remaining slices of bread in the egg and place on top of the ham, buttered side up. Lower the lid and toast for 2 minutes. Serve with grilled tomato halves.

Smoky Brunch
Makes 4   (Pictured on page 63)

The lovely smoky flavour of these Brevilles is equally popular at supper time and breakfast time. Serve them with grilled tomatoes and green peas.

75 g/3 oz smoked cod or haddock fillets
milk
butter
2 eggs, beaten
black pepper
4 slices bread, buttered on one side

Poach the smoked fish fillets in a little milk and butter or follow the directions on the pack for boil-in-the-bag frozen fillets. Drain the fish, retaining some of the liquid, and mash it with a fork. Very lightly scramble the eggs with a little of the cooking liquor from the fish. When the eggs start to set, add the fish and mix well together. Season with pepper. Lay two slices of bread, buttered side down, on the preheated scallops. Divide the egg and fish mixture between the two pieces of bread and top with the remaining bread, buttered side up. Lower the lid and toast for 2 minutes. Serve garnished with parsley sprigs.

Devilled Mushroom Brevilles
Makes 4

Anchovy was a very popular flavouring in Victorian times and its subtle flavour goes particularly well with mushrooms.

2 anchovy fillets *or* 15 ml spoon/1 tablespoon anchovy
    essence
50 g/2 oz butter
4 slices bread
1 small onion, finely chopped
100 g/4 oz mushrooms, finely chopped
5 ml spoon/1 teaspoon tomato ketchup
1.25 ml spoon/¼ teaspoon dry mustard
salt and pepper

If you are using anchovy fillets, rinse them in cold water and rub them through a sieve. Cream the butter and blend with the sieved anchovies or essence. Spread about half of the butter on one side of each slice of bread. Melt the remaining butter in a frying pan. Fry the onion in this until it turns transparent. Add the mushrooms and continue cooking gently until tender. Remove from the heat, drain off any excess liquid, add the remaining ingredients and stir well. Lay two slices of bread, buttered side down, on the preheated scallops. Add the mushroom mixture and top with the remaining slices of bread, buttered side up. Lower the lid and toast for 2 minutes.

Chocolate Bread; Breakfast Brevilles; Smoky Brunch

Chocolate Bread
Makes 4   (Pictured on page 63)

If you like the croissants with chocolate that the French are
so fond of you will certainly like this. I like it even better
with a little jam.

2 × 5 ml spoon/2 teaspoons caster sugar
4 slices bread, buttered on one side
2 large bars chocolate Flake, cut in half
2 × 5 ml spoon/2 teaspoons apricot jam (optional)

Sprinkle the sugar over the buttered sides of the bread and
shake off any loose granules. Place two slices of bread,
sugared side down, on the preheated scallops. Lay half a
Flake bar over each scallop and, if you are using jam, cover
each with 2.5 ml spoon/½ teaspoon of jam. Top with the
remaining bread, sugared side up. Lower the lid and toast
for 2–3 minutes.

Sweet Egg Toasties
Makes 4

These toasties are particularly good on the morning after the
night before!

2 eggs
4 × 5 ml spoon/4 teaspoons sugar
grated orange rind (optional)
4 thick slices white bread, buttered on one side
2 × 15 ml spoon/2 tablespoons of your favourite
    marmalade

Break the eggs into a wide soup bowl and beat with a fork.
Add 2 × 5 ml spoon/2 teaspoons of sugar (and grated
orange rind, if used) and mix well. Press two slices of bread,
buttered side up, into the egg mixture and then lay on the
preheated scallops, buttered side down. Spoon on the marmalade. Dip the remaining pieces of bread in the rest of the

egg and lay them, buttered side up, on top. Lower the lid and toast for 4 minutes.

Kipper Delights
Makes 4

Kippers take on quite a new dimension when treated in this way and even people who are normally worried about the bones eat these Brevilles with enthusiasm.

175 g/6 oz frozen kipper fillets
50 g/2 oz cream cheese
5 ml spoon/1 teaspoon lemon juice
black pepper
4 slices bread, buttered on one side

Cook the kipper fillets as directed on the pack. Drain the fish and remove any skin or bones. Mash with a fork and mix in the cream cheese, lemon juice and black pepper. Lay two slices of bread, buttered side down, on the preheated scallops. Divide the kipper mixture between the two and top with the remaining bread, buttered side up. Lower the lid and toast for 2 minutes.

Bury Breakfast
Makes 4

Black puddings from Bury market are reputed to be the best in Britain and their spicy taste is excellent at breakfast time. In France black pudding is often served with cooked apples and in this recipe I have used this combination.

15 g/½ oz butter
1 small cooking or green eating apple, cored and sliced
175 g/6 oz black pudding, sliced
4 slices bread, buttered on one side
black pepper

Melt the butter in a frying pan and gently fry the apple slices. After a minute or two add the sliced black pudding and fry on each side. Take the pan off the heat and remove the skin from the black pudding. Lay two slices of bread, buttered side down, on the preheated scallops. Arrange the apple and black pudding slices on top. Sprinkle with black pepper and cover with the remaining slices of bread, buttered side up. Lower the lid and toast for 2 minutes.

Stuffed Oatcakes 1
Makes 4

The large, rather floppy Lancashire oatcakes have always been a favourite in my family and they toast beautifully. If you can't find them, use the same filling in pizza dough (see page 68) or samosa dough (see page 73).

1 onion, very finely chopped
15 ml spoon/1 tablespoon cooking oil
4 large lamb's kidneys, very finely chopped
75 g/3 oz mushrooms, very finely chopped
15 ml spoon/1 tablespoon very finely chopped parsley
2.5 ml spoon/½ teaspoon dry mustard
15 ml spoon/1 tablespoon flour
salt and pepper
2–4 oatcakes, depending on size
butter, melted

Fry the onion in cooking oil until it turns transparent. Add the kidneys and mushrooms and continue cooking gently until the mushrooms soften a little. Sprinkle on the parsley, mustard, flour and seasoning. Stir well and cook over a low heat for 15 minutes, stirring from time to time. Cut 4 × 13 cm/5 in squares out of the oatcakes and brush one side of each with melted butter. Lay two pieces of oatcake, buttered side down, on the preheated scallops. Divide the kidney mixture between the two and top with the remaining pieces of oatcake, buttered side up. Lower the lid and toast for 2–3 minutes until crisp.

Stuffed Oatcakes 2
Makes 4

100 g/4 oz Lancashire or Wensleydale cheese, grated
3 × 15 ml spoon/3 tablespoons canned or homemade apple
   purée
pinch of sage
2–4 oatcakes, depending on size
butter, melted

Mix the cheese and apple purée and stir in the sage. Cut
4 × 13 cm/5 in squares out of the oatcakes and brush one
side of each with melted butter. Lay two pieces of oatcake,
buttered side down, on the preheated scallops. Divide the
cheese and apple mixture between the two and top with the
remaining oatcakes, buttered side up. Lower the lid and
toast for 2–3 minutes until crisp.

Pizzas, Pastries and Pasties

The recipes in this section use either dough or pastry linings rather than bread and will show you how to create still more variety using your sandwich toaster.

PIZZA DOUGH
Pizza dough makes a really unusual lining for Brevilles and it comes out deliciously crisp and crunchy. Make the dough an hour or so before you want it and leave it to rise in a warm place.

Basic Pizza Dough
Makes enough for 8–10 Brevilles

15 g/½ oz fresh yeast *or* 2 × 5 ml spoon/2 teaspoons dried
    yeast mixed with 5 ml spoon/1 teaspoon sugar
350 ml/12 fl oz lukewarm water
450 g/1 lb brown or white flour
salt

Mix the yeast or yeast and sugar with the lukewarm water. If using fresh yeast, cream to a very thin paste. If using dried yeast, leave to stand for about 15–20 minutes until the mixture is frothy. Sift the flour into a large bowl and add the salt. Make a well in the centre and pour in the yeast mixture. Mix to a stiff dough. Flour a flat surface and knead the dough on this for at least 5–8 minutes until it is smooth and elastic. Place in an oiled polythene bag and leave in a warm place to rise for about 45 minutes or until it has doubled in size.

Basic Tomato Sauce
Makes about 10 × 15 ml spoon/10 tablespoons

1 onion, finely chopped
15 ml spoon/1 tablespoon cooking oil
226 g/8 oz can tomatoes
15 ml spoon/1 tablespoon tomato purée
salt and pepper
pinch of thyme, oregano or mixed herbs

Fry the onion in cooking oil until it turns transparent. Add
the remaining ingredients and bring to the boil. Simmer for
about 30 minutes or until the sauce is fairly thick. Sieve or
blend and leave to cool.

Vesuvio
Makes 8

1 quantity Basic Pizza Dough (see page 68)
cooking oil
4 × 15 ml spoon/4 tablespoons Basic Tomato Sauce (see
  above)
16 slices salami
100 g/4 oz cheddar cheese, grated
16 stoned olives, halved
salt and pepper

Roll out the pizza dough until it is as thin as you can get it
and leave it to rest for 5 minutes. Cut the dough into
8 × 13 cm/5 in squares and brush one side of each with
cooking oil. Lay two or four of them on the preheated
scallops. Quickly brush with tomato sauce and arrange
slices of salami, grated cheese and halved olives on the top.
Season to taste. Brush the other side of the remaining oiled
pizza squares with tomato sauce and lay, oiled side up, on
the top. Lower the lid and toast for about 3–4 minutes until
golden brown and crisp. Repeat with the remaining ingredients if necessary.

Capri

Makes 8

1 quantity Basic Pizza Dough (see page 68)
cooking oil
4 × 15 ml spoon/4 tablespoons Basic Tomato Sauce (see page 69)
4 × 15 ml spoon/4 tablespoons crushed pineapple, well drained
4 slices cooked ham, approx. 10 cm/4 in square
100 g/4 oz Mozzarella cheese, sliced
black pepper

Roll out the pizza dough until it is as thin as you can get it and leave it to rest for 5 minutes. Cut the dough into 8 × 13 cm/5 in squares and brush one side of each with cooking oil. Lay two or four of them, oiled side down, on the preheated scallops and brush with tomato sauce. Place 3 × 2.5 ml spoon/1½ teaspoon of crushed pineapple on each scallop and arrange a slice of ham and slices of cheese on top. Season to taste. Brush the unoiled sides of the remaining squares with tomato sauce and lay on top, oiled side up. Lower the lid and toast for 3–4 minutes until golden brown and crispy. Repeat with the remaining ingredients if necessary.

Pompeii

Makes 8

1 quantity Basic Pizza Dough (see page 68)
198 g/7 oz can tuna, drained
50 g/1¾ oz can anchovy fillets, drained
2 small tomatoes, finely chopped
salt or celery salt and pepper
cooking oil
4 × 15 ml spoon/4 tablespoons Basic Tomato Sauce (see page 69)

Capri Pizzas

Roll out the pizza dough until it is as thin as you can get it and leave it to rest for 5 minutes. Mash the tuna and anchovies together in a basin and add the chopped tomato and seasonings. Cut the pizza dough into 8 × 13 cm/5 in squares and brush one side of each with cooking oil. Lay two or four of them, oiled side down, on the preheated scallops and brush with tomato sauce. Spoon on the tuna and anchovy mixture. Brush the unoiled sides of the remaining squares with tomato sauce and lay on top, oiled side up. Lower the lid and toast for 3–4 minutes until crisp and golden brown. Repeat with the remaining ingredients if necessary.

Milano
Makes 8

1 quantity Basic Pizza Dough (see page 68)
15 g/½ oz butter
1 small onion, finely chopped
1 clove garlic, finely chopped
½ small green pepper, shredded
100 g/4 oz mushrooms, sliced
5 ml spoon/1 teaspoon oregano
salt and pepper
cooking oil
4 × 15 ml spoon/4 tablespoons Basic Tomato Sauce (see page 69)

Roll out the pizza dough until it is as thin as you can get it and leave it to rest for 5 minutes. Melt the butter in a pan and gently fry the onion and garlic. After 1–2 minutes add the green pepper, mushrooms and oregano and season to taste. Continue cooking for about 5 minutes. Cut the pizza dough into 8 × 13 cm/5 in squares and brush one side of each with cooking oil. Lay two or four of them, oiled side down, on the preheated scallops and brush with tomato sauce. Spoon the onion and pepper mixture on the top. Brush the unoiled side of the remaining squares with tomato sauce and lay on top, oiled side up. Lower the lid and toast for 3–4 minutes until golden brown and crisp. Repeat with the remaining ingredients if necessary.

SAMOSA DOUGH

Samosa dough is a very quickly prepared dough which is quite low in fat. It is popular in India and South-east Asia generally. In China a similar dough is used to make spring rolls. In most of these countries the little packets of food are deep fried, but the pastry cooks to a very nice crisp finish in both the SG3 Snack 'n' Sandwich Toaster and the 8–Up Snack 'n' Sandwich Toaster. It is important to fill the samosas really full as this helps to press the pastry against both sides of the scallops.

Basic Samosa Dough
Makes 4

100 g/4 oz plain flour
salt
25 g/1 oz butter
3 × 15 ml spoon/3 tablespoons milk

Sift the flour and salt into a bowl. Heat the butter and milk gently until the butter melts. Pour over the flour and work to a smooth dough. Break the dough into four pieces and roll out to 4 × 13 cm/5 in squares.

Bombay
Makes 4   (Pictured on page 75)

1 small onion, finely chopped
2 × 15 ml spoon/2 tablespoons cooking oil
1–2 × 15 ml spoon/1–2 tablespoons curry powder to taste
100 g/4 oz cooked peas
100 g/4 oz cooked potatoes, diced
213 g/7½ oz can minced beef with onions
1 quantity Basic Samosa Dough (see above)
butter or cooking oil

Fry the onion in half the cooking oil with the curry powder. After about 5 minutes add the peas and potatoes and toss

73

over a low heat for a further 1–2 minutes. Add the minced beef and keep on one side. Roll out the samosa dough squares and brush one side of each with butter or cooking oil. Lay two of the squares, buttered side down, on the preheated scallops. Pile up the curried mixture over the scallops and cover with the remaining squares, buttered side up. Lower the lid without latching and cook for about 4 minutes until crisp.

Peking
Makes 4

¼ cooked chicken (approx. 175 g/6 oz chicken meat)
100 g/4 oz bean sprouts, fresh or canned
2 × 5 ml spoon/2 teaspoons soya sauce
pinch of 5-spice powder *or* a little finely chopped root ginger (optional)
salt and pepper
1 quantity Basic Samosa Dough (see page 73)
butter or cooking oil

Cut the chicken meat into small, thin strips. Blanch fresh bean sprouts by pouring boiling water over them. Drain blanched or canned sprouts very well and mix with the prepared chicken, soya sauce, spice powder or ginger if used, and seasoning. Spread one side of the samosa dough squares with butter or cooking oil and place two squares, buttered side down, on the preheated scallops. Pile up the chicken mixture over the scallops and cover with the remaining squares, buttered side up. Lower the lid without latching and cook for about 4 minutes until crisp.

Samosas: Peking; Bombay

Singapore
Makes 4

1 clove garlic, crushed
1.25 ml spoon/¼ teaspoon ground chilli powder
2 × 5 ml spoon/2 teaspoons cooking oil
2 × 15 ml spoon/2 tablespoons peanut butter
2 × 5 ml spoon/2 teaspoons lemon juice
75–100 ml/3–4 fl oz chicken stock
pinch of sugar
2 × 5 ml spoon/2 teaspoons soya sauce
275 g/10 oz cold cooked lamb, chicken or turkey, minced
  or chopped very finely
1 quantity Basic Samosa Dough (see page 73)
butter or cooking oil

Fry the garlic and chilli powder in the cooking oil for a
minute or so. Mix the peanut butter, lemon juice and sufficient stock to form a smooth cream. Pour into the pan with
the garlic and chilli and bring to the boil. Add the sugar,
soya sauce and meat and keep on one side. Roll out the
samosa dough and spread one side of each square with
butter or cooking oil. Lay two of the squares, buttered side
down, on the preheated scallops and pile on the peanut and
meat mixture. Cover with the remaining squares of dough,
buttered side up. Lower the lid without latching and cook
for about 4 minutes until crisp.

SHORTCRUST AND PUFF PASTRY
Both shortcrust and puff pastry cook very satisfactorily in
the Breville Snack 'n' Sandwich Toaster. There are two
points to remember: first, the pastry tends to shrink when it
comes into contact with the hot scallops and so the squares
need to be cut slightly larger to compensate for this, and
second, the handles of the appliance should not be latched
together.

Roll out the pastry fairly thinly and make sure that the
filling is cut finely enough to prevent pieces piercing the
pastry. Brush the pastry with melted butter or oil and place
this greased side of the pastry against the scallops.

Salmon Pasties
Makes 4   (Pictured on page 79)

These delicious pasties are equally popular for Sunday supper and as cocktail sandwiches. If you want the smaller,
daintier snacks, turn each pasty once during cooking.

200 g/7 oz canned or fresh salmon
4 spring onions, finely chopped
2 × 15 ml spoon/2 tablespoons finely chopped parsley
15 ml spoon/1 tablespoon mayonnaise
salt and pepper
175 g/6 oz puff pastry
melted butter or cooking oil

Drain the salmon if canned and mash the flesh with a fork.
Add the spring onions, parsley, mayonnaise and seasoning
and mix well together. Roll out the pastry to approximately
26 cm/10 in square and cut into four smaller squares. Brush
with melted butter or cooking oil and lay two, oiled side
down, on the preheated scallops. Quickly fill with the salmon mixture and cover with the remaining pastry squares,
oiled side up. Lower the lid without latching and cook for
3–4 minutes, checking after 3 minutes to see that the pastry
is not burning.

Cock-a-leekie Pies
Makes 4

These little pies can be eaten as a snack, but they also make
an excellent starter for a dinner party. In the latter case serve
them with a piquant sauce.

2 small leeks (75 g/3 oz), finely sliced
15 g/½ oz butter
100 g/4 oz cooked chicken, finely chopped
15 ml spoon/1 tablespoon thick yogurt or cottage cheese
salt and pepper
175 g/6 oz shortcrust pastry
cooking oil

Gently fry the leeks in butter until soft. Mix with the cooked chicken, yogurt or cottage cheese and seasoning. Roll out the pastry to approximately 26 cm/10 in square and cut into four smaller squares. Brush one side of the pastry with oil and place two of the squares, oiled side down, on the pre-heated scallops. Spoon on the chicken mixture and cover with the remaining squares of pastry, oiled side up. Lower the lid without latching and cook for 4 minutes until the pastry is cooked. Serve at once.

Morecambe Magic
Makes 4

Morecambe Bay shrimps have always been considered a special treat in my family and the quick cooking of the Breville Snack 'n' Sandwich Toaster ensures that they remain at their best.

2 × 50 g/1¾ oz pots frozen potted shrimps
1 tomato, finely chopped
25 g/1 oz grated cheese
salt and pepper
175 g/6 oz puff pastry

Take the butter off the top of the shrimps and melt it in a saucer over hot water. Mix the shrimps with the tomato, cheese and seasonings. Roll out the pastry to approximately 26 cm/10 in square and cut into four smaller squares. Brush with the melted shrimp butter. Lay two pastry squares, buttered side down, on the preheated scallops and quickly fill with the shrimp mixture. Cover with the remaining pastry squares, buttered side up. Lower the lid without latching and cook for 3–4 minutes, checking after 3 minutes to see that the pastry is not burning.

Morecambe Magic; Apple Pies; Salmon Pasties

Cornish Pasties
Makes 4

Served with baked beans and a green vegetable, these substantial Brevilles can turn from a snack into a full meal.
Incidently, it's worth remembering that the same filling can
also be used with a buttered bread lining.

213 g/7½ oz can minced beef with onions
225 g/8 oz cooked potatoes, diced
1.25 ml spoon/¼ teaspoon dried marjoram
salt and pepper
175 g/6 oz shortcrust pastry
cooking oil

Mix the minced beef, potatoes, marjoram and seasonings in
a bowl. Roll out the pastry to approximately 26 cm/10 in
square and cut into four smaller squares. Brush one side of
each square with oil and place two of them, oiled side down,
on the preheated scallops. Spoon on the beef and potato
mixture and cover with the remaining pastry squares, oiled
side up. Lower the lid without latching and cook for 4
minutes until the pastry is cooked through. Serve at once.

Apple Pies
Makes 4   (Pictured on page 79)

Any kind of chopped or cooked fruit purée can be used as a
filling for these pies.

1 large or 2 small eating apples, cored and grated on the
   finest mesh
15 ml spoon/1 tablespoon raisins
5 ml spoon/1 teaspoon ground cinnamon
2 × 5 ml spoon/2 teaspoons double cream
approx. 15 ml spoon/1 tablespoon brown or white sugar to
   taste
175 g/6 oz puff pastry
melted butter
icing sugar

Mix the grated apple, raisins, cinnamon, cream and sugar. Roll out the pastry to approximately 26 cm/10 in square and cut into four smaller squares. Brush with melted butter and lay two pieces of pastry, buttered side down, on the pre-heated scallops. Quickly fill with the apple mixture and cover with the remaining pastry squares, buttered side up. Lower the lid without latching and cook for 3–4 minutes, checking after 3 minutes to see that the pastry is not burning. Dust with icing sugar before serving.

CHOUX PASTRY

Choux pastry is quick and easy to make and there is no resting time or rolling out to worry about. It cooks to a lovely light texture in the Breville Snack 'n' Sandwich Toaster and can be eaten hot or cold.

Basic Choux Pastry

Makes enough for 12 choux pastry Brevilles

125 ml/4 fl oz water
40 g/1½ oz butter
50 g/2 oz plain flour
pinch of salt
2 large eggs (size 1 or 2)

Heat the water and butter in a pan. Add the flour and salt when the mixture boils and the butter has melted completely. Beat over the heat with a wooden spoon for 1–2 minutes. Remove from the heat. Beat in the eggs, one at a time and continue beating until the mixture is smooth and shiny.

Hot Choux Melba

Makes 12

1 quantity Basic Choux Pastry (see above)
fruit (optional)
12 small scoops vanilla ice cream
hot chocolate sauce *or* maple syrup

Place 15 ml spoon/1 tablespoon of the basic choux pastry mixture on each of the preheated scallops. Lower the lid and cook for about 8–10 minutes. Remove from the toaster, split and fill with fruit and ice cream. Repeat with the remaining pastry. Top with hot chocolate sauce or maple syrup and serve at once.

Savoury Choux Rolls
Makes 12

1 quantity Basic Choux Pastry (see page 81)
300 ml/½ pint white sauce
diced cooked chicken, prawns, cooked mushroom, diced
    ham and peas or chopped asparagus
salt and pepper

Place 15 ml/1 tablespoon of the basic choux pastry mixture on each of the preheated scallops. Lower the lid and cook for about 8–10 minutes. Meanwhile, heat the white sauce, add the filling of your choice and season to taste. Remove the choux rolls from the toaster, split and fill with the sauce. Serve at once. Repeat with the remaining ingredients.
    Asparagus Choux Rolls are pictured opposite.

Choux Splits
Makes 12

1 quantity Basic Choux Pastry (see page 81)
300 ml/½ pint whipping cream
2 × 5 ml spoon/2 teaspoons sugar
few drops of vanilla essence
fresh fruit or raspberry jam
icing sugar

Asparagus Choux Rolls

Place 15 ml spoon/1 tablespoon of the basic choux pastry mixture on each of the preheated scallops. Lower the lid and cook for about 8–10 minutes. Remove from the toaster, split and leave to cool. Repeat with the remaining pastry. Whisk the cream, sugar and vanilla essence until stiff. Just before serving, place some fruit or 5 ml spoon/1 teaspoon of raspberry jam and 15 ml spoon/1 tablespoon of cream in each split. Sprinkle the top with a little icing sugar.

Strawberry Choux Splits are pictured on the back cover.

Party Specials

TOASTED COCKTAIL SANDWICHES
These sandwiches are half the size of standard Brevilles and I
find that they are very popular at parties. Prepare the sandwiches in the normal way using any of the fillings. Use the
SG3 Snack 'n' Sandwich Toaster or the 8-Up Snack 'n'
Sandwich Toaster. After the sandwiches have been toasting
for 1 minute, turn them so that they lie across the cutters and
lower the lid again to finish cooking. This divides each
standard-size Breville into two. If you find that these smaller sandwiches tend to burst, you should use less filling in
the next batch.

Prawn and Avocado Canapés
Makes 16   (Pictured on page 87)

Don't be shy of the lemon juice in this recipe – it is necessary
to keep the avocado from discolouring and it also adds a
piquant flavour to the mixture.

2 avocado pears, stoned and peeled
juice of 1 lemon
200 g/7 oz peeled prawns
salt and black pepper
8 slices of bread, buttered on one side

Mash the avocados with a fork and sieve or blend with the
lemon juice. Mix in the prawns and seasoning. Lay two or
four slices of bread, buttered side down, over the preheated
scallops. Spoon the avocado and prawn mixture over the
top and cover with slices of bread, buttered side up. Lower

the lid and toast for 1 minute. Raise the lid and turn the Brevilles so that they lie across the cutting bars. Lower the lid and toast for 1 minute more. Repeat with the remaining ingredients if necessary. Serve garnished with wedges of lemon or with prawns and slices of avocado.

Smoked Salmon and Egg Canapés
Makes 16

Smoked salmon adds a touch of class to any drinks party and the combination of smoked salmon and egg is a classic one.

15 ml spoon/1 tablespoon milk
15 g/½ oz butter
4 eggs, beaten
75 g/3 oz smoked salmon, chopped
salt and pepper
8 slices bread, buttered on one side

Heat the milk and butter in a pan and add the eggs. Scramble until just set. Add the smoked salmon and seasoning. Lay two or four slices of bread, buttered side down, on the preheated scallops. Add a heaped tablespoonful of the smoked salmon mixture to each scallop and cover with slices of bread, buttered side up. Lower the lid and toast for 1 minute. Raise the lid and arrange the Brevilles so that they lie across the cutting bars. Lower the lid again and toast for 1 minute more. Repeat with the remaining ingredients if necessary. Serve garnished with wedges of lemon or a little scrambled egg and smoked salmon.

Duck and Orange Canapés
Makes 16

This is a recipe for really special occasions. Cook the duck in advance and eat the breast hot, retaining the leg meat for the canapés. Alternatively, buy a good duck paté or terrine.

Duck and Orange Canapés; Prawn and Avocado Canapés; Smoked Salmon and Egg Canapés

8 slices bread, buttered on one side
225 g/8 oz cooked duck or duck paté, cut into thin slices
2 small oranges, peeled and segmented, *or* 213 g/7½ oz can
 mandarin oranges, well drained
2 × 15 ml spoon/2 tablespoons mayonnaise
2 sprigs mint, broken into pieces

Lay two or four slices of bread, buttered side down, on the
preheated scallops. Arrange a few slices of duck and a seg-
ment of fresh orange or 2–3 mandarin segments on each
scallop. Add a little mayonnaise and a piece of mint. Cover
with slices of bread, buttered side up. Lower the lid and
toast for 1 minute. Lift the lid and rearrange the canapés
across the cutting bars. Lower the lid again and toast for
another minute. Repeat with the remaining ingredients if
necessary. Serve garnished with wedges of orange or a small
slice of duck and a piece of orange.

Chicken Liver Canapés
Makes 16   (Pictured on page 95)

Devils on Horseback is the colourful name given to chicken
livers rolled in bacon and these are always in demand at
parties. For a change, place a stoned prune, a couple of
smoked mussels or half an artichoke heart in the bacon roll.

8 rashers bacon
350 g/12 oz chicken livers
40 g/1½ oz butter
salt and pepper
5 ml spoon/1 teaspoon mixed herbs or powdered bouquet
 garni
8 slices bread

Fry or grill the bacon and cut in half lengthways. Gently fry
the chicken livers in 15 g/½ oz butter until just cooked
through. Season to taste. Mix the remaining butter with the
mixed herbs and spread on one side of each slice of bread.

Roll each strip of bacon round some of the chicken livers to make 16 rolls. Lay two or four slices of bread, buttered side down, on the preheated scallops. Arrange two bacon rolls on each scallop. Cover with slices of bread, buttered side up. Lower the lid and toast for 1 minute. Open the lid and rearrange the sandwiches across the cutting bars to make 16 canapés. Lower the lid and toast for another minute. Repeat with the remaining ingredients if necessary.

Smoky Gems
Makes 24

The cheese in these delicious Gems tends to make them rather runny, so serve napkins and warn your guests of the problem or your carpet may suffer!

175 g/6 oz smoked cod or haddock fillets
300 ml/½ pint milk
50 g/2 oz butter
60 g/2½ oz flour
100 g/4 oz Camembert cheese, finely chopped
salt and pepper
12 slices bread, buttered on one side

Poach the smoked fish in a little of the milk or follow the directions on the pack for boil-in-the-bag frozen fillets. Drain, retaining the liquid, and mash with a fork. Melt the butter in a pan and stir in the flour. Gradually add the liquid from the fish and the remaining milk, stirring all the time. When the mixture boils add the fish, cheese and seasoning. Lay two or four slices of bread, buttered side down, on the preheated scallops. Add 15 ml spoon/1 tablespoon of the smoked fish mixture to each scallop and cover with slices of bread, buttered side up. Lower the lid and toast for 1 minute. Raise the lid and rearrange the Brevilles across the cutting bars. Lower the lid again and toast for a further minute. Repeat with the remaining slices of bread and serve garnished with sprigs of parsley.

SAVOURY WHIRLS

These are also useful for parties or to serve with pre-dinner drinks. Prepare the whirls in advance and cook them just before serving. Start by trimming the crusts from the bread and then flatten each slice with a rolling pin. Spread with the chosen filling and roll up. Store until required. If necessary, brush the rolls with melted butter and place along the pre-heated scallops of the 8-Up Snack 'n' Sandwich Toaster or diagonally along the scallops of the SG3 Snack 'n' Sandwich Toaster. Make sure in each case that the join of the roll rests against the cutter. Lower the lid and toast for 1 minute. Check the whirls after this time and turn them if necessary to ensure even cooking before you continue toasting. If you want small whirls, turn the rolls across the cutters and then lower the lid and continue toasting. All the flavoured butters mentioned on pages 11–12 can be used for whirls, but take care not to use too much butter. Do not use runny fillings in these whirls.

Garlic and Parsley Whirls
Makes 16

These fragrant whirls are particularly good made with wholemeal bread, but do make sure that the bread is absolutely fresh or it will not roll up easily.

100 g/4 oz cream cheese
3–4 cloves garlic to taste, crushed
8 × 15 ml spoon/8 tablespoons very finely chopped parsley
8 slices bread, buttered on one side

Mix the cream cheese, garlic and parsley to a smooth paste and spread over the unbuttered side of the bread. Roll up each slice of bread, buttered side out, and place one on each of the preheated scallops. Lower the lid and toast for 2–3 minutes. Repeat with the remaining rolls if necessary.

Garlic and Parsley Whirls

Liver and Sage Whirls
Makes 16   (Pictured on the back cover)

I use home-made liver pâté for this recipe but you could use
liver sausage or indeed any kind of smooth pâté. For a
change, experiment with different herbs.

175 g/6 oz liver pâté
2 × 5 ml spoon/2 teaspoons dried sage *or* 15 ml spoon/1
    tablespoon freshly chopped sage
8 slices bread, buttered on one side

Mix the liver pâté and sage to a smooth paste and spread
over the unbuttered side of the bread. Roll up each slice of
bread, buttered side out, and place one on each of the
preheated scallops. Lower the lid and toast for 1 minute. Lift
the lid and rearrange the whirls across the cutting bars.
Replace the lid and toast for 1–2 minutes more. Repeat with
the remaining rolls if necessary.

Smoky Whirls
Makes 16

If you cannot find any smoked cod's roe, try substituting
smoked mackerel or buckling.

75 g/3 oz smoked cod's roe
75 g/3 oz cream cheese
a little lemon juice
black pepper
8 slices bread, buttered on one side

Mix the cod's roe, cream cheese, lemon juice and black
pepper to a smooth paste and spread over the unbuttered
side of the bread. Roll up each slice of bread, buttered side
out, and lay one on each of the preheated scallops. Lower the
lid and toast for 1 minute. Lift the lid and rearrange the

whirls across the cutting bars. Replace the lid and toast for 1–2 minutes more. Repeat with the remaining rolls if necessary.

Spiced Herring Whirls
Makes 16

Rollmops are the easiest kind of herring to use in these whirls but the various kinds of canned marinated herring from Scandinavia are also very good.

1–2 rollmop herrings (150 g/5 oz)
2–3 shallots or spring onions
2–3 drops Tabasco *or* pinch of cayenne pepper
8 slices bread, buttered on one side

Remove any fins from the rollmops. Mince the fish with the onion. Mix in the Tabasco or cayenne and spread over the unbuttered side of the bread. Roll up each slice of bread, buttered side out, and place one on each of the preheated scallops. Lower the lid and toast for 1 minute. Lift the lid and rearrange the whirls across the cutting bars. Replace the lid and toast for 1–2 minutes more. Repeat with the remaining rolls if necessary.

MORE SUBSTANTIAL FINGERS

Asparagus Fingers
Makes 8

These make delicious and quite substantial party snacks. Do be sure to buy a good brand of asparagus – the extra money that may be involved is well worth it to ensure really tender spears.

250 g/8¾ oz can asparagus tips, well drained
8 slices bread, buttered on one side
4 × 15 ml spoon/4 tablespoons hollandaise sauce or
  mayonnaise

Cut the asparagus spears to fit the length of the Breville
scallops. If you are using an SG3 Snack 'n' Sandwich Toaster rather than an 8-Up Snack 'n' Sandwich Toaster, you
may need to cut the spears to different lengths to fit the
triangular shape of the scallops. Lay two or four slices of
bread, buttered side down, on the preheated scallops.
Arrange the asparagus over the scallops and spread
2 × 5 ml spoon/2 teaspoons of sauce or mayonnaise over
each cluster of asparagus. Top with slices of bread, buttered
side up. Lower the lid and toast for 2 minutes. Repeat with
the remaining ingredients if necessary.

Mock Caviare Fingers
Makes 8

These fishy Brevilles make an exotic party snack. They can
also be turned once during cooking to make small cocktail
sandwiches.

4 hard-boiled eggs, finely chopped
2 × 15 ml spoon/2 tablespoons lumpfish roe or smoked
  cod's roe
4 × 15 ml spoon/4 tablespoons tartare sauce
8 slices of bread, buttered on one side

Mix the hard-boiled eggs, fish roe and tartare sauce in a
basin. Lay two or four slices of bread, buttered side down,
on the preheated scallops. Spoon on the egg mixture and
cover with more bread, buttered side up. Lower the lid and
toast for 2 minutes. Repeat with the remaining ingredients if
necessary.

Chicken Liver Canapés

Breville Kebabs
Makes 8

This is another fairly substantial party snack. It is easier to make in the 8-Up Snack 'n' Sandwich Toaster but it can be made in the SG3 Snack 'n' Sandwich Toaster by cutting and arranging the chopped chicken and pepper slices to fit the triangular shape of the scallops. In either case, the more piquant the barbecue sauce you can find the better.

1 green pepper, halved and seeded
½ small chicken, boned
8 slices bread, buttered on one side
8 × 5 ml spoon/8 teaspoons barbecue sauce

Place the green pepper halves in boiling water and cook for about 8–10 minutes until tender. Cut into small squares. Cut the chicken into small chunks to fit the scallops. Lay two or four slices of bread, buttered side down, on the preheated scallops. Arrange alternate pieces of chicken and green pepper along the length of each scallop and top with 5 ml spoon/1 teaspoon of barbecue sauce. Cover with slices of bread, buttered side up, lower the lid and toast for 2 minutes. Repeat with the remaining ingredients if necessary. Serve with extra barbecue sauce as a dip.